TopReaders

Jungle Life

Denise Ryan

Contents

Jungles are dense ,
warm, and wet forests.
Let's find out what
lives there.

In the Trees

Many jungle animals
live high up in the trees.
They howl, chirp, call,
and sing as they move
through the branches.

Can you find the monkeys?
Can you find the macaws ?
Can you find the toucan
and the quetzal ?

On the Jungle Floor

Moss and fungi grow on this dead jungle tree. Tiny animals feed on the plants.

spider

moss

fungi

ants

seedling

fungi

Insect-eating Plants

Some jungle plants eat insects.
Sticky leaves and hairs trap
the insects. When the insects die,
the plant eats them.

insect

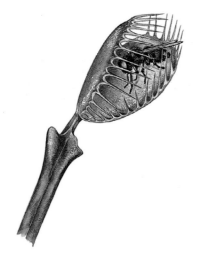

Venus flytrap

trapped insects

poison frog
tadpole

velvet worm

alligator lizard

snail

ant

Living in a Plant

Bromeliads grow high in jungle trees. Rain makes pools in the bowl-shaped leaves. Animals gather in the plant to drink and eat.

poison frog

mouse opposum

How many animals are living in this bromeliad?

young python

Changing Colors

Green tree pythons are yellow or brown when they hatch. They turn green when they become adults.

adult python

Tree pythons live in northern Australia and New Guinea.

Jungle Birds

Many birds live in the jungles of South America. Some have bright colors but they can be hard to see in the dappled sunlight.

macaw

aracari

trogon

harpy eagle

Claws

Harpy eagles swoop down
on monkeys in the
forest trees. They grab
the monkeys in
their sharp claws .

The surprised
howler monkey
cannot escape
the harpy eagle.

The eagle's feet are as big as a man's hands.

Showing Off

Colorful birds of paradise live
in the jungles of New Guinea.

female

The males have long feathers
that spread out from their bodies.
They dance to attract female birds.

male

Swingers

Monkeys live in jungles in Africa, Asia, and America. South American spider monkeys use their tails to swing from tree to tree.

These monkeys eat fruit that they pick from the trees.

The baby spider monkey wraps its tail around its mother. It doesn't want to fall off!

Moving Along

Orangutans live in trees in the jungles of Asia. They move through the trees by swinging from branch to branch.

Orangutans have strong hands and feet that grasp and hold branches.

They have very long arms, short legs, and no tail.

Hanging Around

These three unusual animals
grip tree branches with
their special tails. They live
in Central and South America.

tree
porcupine

tamandua

kinkajou

The animals hang on to branches with their tails and use their hands to gather food.

Huge Mouth

Pythons can swallow big animals.
They slowly wind themselves around
their prey and move their jaws over it.

This python is eating a wild pig—head first!

The Jungle at Night

After dark, many animals wake up and search for food on the jungle floor.

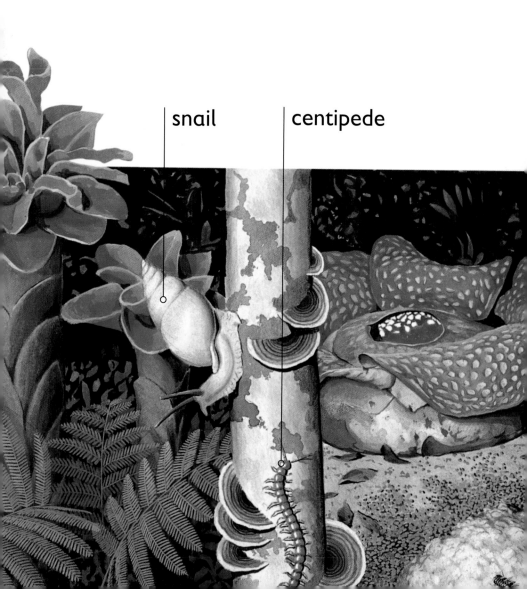

snail

centipede

The spotted cuscus lives in trees. It eats leaves and fruit, lizards and insects.

spotted cuscus

python

Quiz

Can you match each animal with its name?

orangutan

toucan

bird of paradise

tamandua

Glossary

bromeliads: kinds of plants that grow on another plant or tree

claws: hard, sharp, curved nails

dappled: with patterns made by the sun

dense: closely packed together

fungi: plants like mushrooms and toadstools

grasp: to grab tightly

macaws: brightly colored parrots

orangutans: large apes that live in Asia

prey: animals that other animals catch and kill for food

quetzal: a bird with a long, colorful tail

seedling: small, new plant

toucan: a black and yellow bird with a long, sharp bill

Index